CW00430358

The
Perfect
Report

THE PERFECT SERIES

ALL YOU NEED TO GET IT RIGHT FIRST TIME

OTHER TITLES IN THE SERIES:

The Perfect Report

ALL YOU NEED
TO GET IT RIGHT
FIRST TIME

PETER BARTRAM

ARROW
BUSINESS BOOKS

Published by Arrow Books in 1994

1 3 5 7 9 10 8 6 4 2

First published by
Arrow Books Limited
20 Vauxhall Bridge Road, London SW1V 2SA

Random House Australia (Pty) Limited
20 Alfred Street, Milsons Point, Sydney
New South Wales 2061, Australia

Random House New Zealand Limited
18 Poland Road, Glenfield
Auckland 10, New Zealand

Random House South Africa (Pty) Limited
PO Box 337, Bergvlei, South Africa

Random House UK Limited Reg. No. 954009
ISBN 0-7126-5907-2

Set in Bembo by
SX Composing Ltd., Rayleigh, Essex
Printed and bound in Great Britain by
Cox and Wyman Ltd, Reading, Berks

ABOUT THE AUTHOR

Peter Bartram

Peter Bartram is a well known journalist and business writer.

He is the author of 14 books, including *Perfect Business Writing* in this series, and several thousand magazine and newspaper articles.

CONTENTS

THE PURPOSE OF THE REPORT

WHAT IS A REPORT?

In the world of business writing the term 'report' has a special kind of aura that other documents don't. The word 'report' on the cover page of a document immediately invests the contents with a special authority. For a report implies that the contents are the product of careful research, mature thought and measured expression. In companies, public bodies and voluntary organizations people take decisions, sometimes important decisions affecting the lives of people or the expenditure of millions, based on the contents of reports. When they have to consider an issue they will often call for a report. The contents of the report will colour their judgement of the matter under consideration and influence their decision. In short, the report is a very special piece of work-related writing which has a status far removed from other business writing, such as letters and memoranda.

The dictionary definition of a report tells only half the story. A report is 'a formal statement of the results of an investigation, or of any matter on which definite information is required, made by some body or person required to do so.' (*Shorter Oxford English Dictionary*). It is what the dictionary definition implies, rather than what it says directly, that is important for the report writer. It suggests that the report is an especially careful piece of work in which facts have been meticulously collected, opinions considered in a balanced way, and conclusions reported in a sober but unambiguous language.

Of course, not all reports carry equal weight. There are

large reports (such as some of those produced by House of Commons Select Committees) and small reports (such as the couple of paragraphs a manager might draft in answer to a simple query). There are mightily influential reports (such as the Beveridge Report of 1944 which mapped out the structure of the modern welfare state) and reports that don't receive a second thought (such as a product faults summary received by managers in a US manufacturing company which always showed zero in every column – because the company no longer made the products). There are reports assembled as the result of the work of a team of people over a long period of time (such as the report of an investigation into a major accident) and reports penned by an individual in a couple of hours (such as a large number of simple management reports turned out in companies every day). The report is not an animal but a species.

Like other species, members of the report family have the same characteristics:

- *A clear purpose.* A report is normally commissioned with a clear aim in mind. However, the purpose could be one of several. We return to this point below.

- *A methodical approach.* A report approaches its subject matter in a logical and methodical way. There is no 'right' way to structure a report, but normally a report could include any or all of the following: an introduction that states the purpose of the report, a section that describes how the report writer or writers went about their business, a description of the evidence collected, a summary of the findings, and a set of recommendations. All these will normally be presented in a sequential way, one following logically upon the other. There are other features which could also appear in some reports and which we will address later.

- *A special tone of language.* Because a report has a purpose, the language used in it is chosen to suit that purpose. Generally, a report is written in language which engages the report's readers at a level they are likely to find appropriate. There is no one writing style that is appropriate to every kind of report. For example, a report of the investigation into a factory death would be written in sober terms and would not be expected to carry any flashes of humour. But a report based on a survey of people's weekend leisure activities could be written with a lighter touch and might contain some well judged sparks of humour. Whatever writing style is chosen, the language of a report should be clear and unambiguous. It should also seek to engage the reader and, where appropriate, win him round to the writer's point of view. We shall return to the subject of report language in more depth later in this book.

As we have seen, the report is a species rather than a single animal. It can range from a single-sided document at one end of the scale to a multi-volumed publication with thousands of pages, perhaps the result of a government investigation, at the other. In between come the bulk of reports – perhaps a dozen pages long, perhaps as many as a couple of hundred pages. It is these reports in between, rather than the two extremes of the single-sided or the multi-volumed, that we are chiefly concerned with in this book. They account for a large proportion of all reports written.

The first point to consider is the different purposes which a report might have.

Defining a report's purpose

Every report is written for a particular reason. So, in that sense, every report has a unique purpose and it is essential that you, as the writer, understand the precise purpose before you embark on the research, compilation and writing of the report. However, while every report has a unique purpose, it is possible to categorize general areas of purpose into which most reports fall. Understanding these different purposes helps your report writing by providing an understanding and framework in which you can approach each unique task.

There are seven main purposes about which you should be aware.

1. *To provide information.* In a sense, all reports provide information but, as we shall see below, the purpose of some reports goes beyond that of straightforward information delivery. There is a specific category of report, however, whose purpose is only information provision.

    Consider, for example, a progress report on a new building project. There could, in fact, be several different types of progress report for different managers involved in various aspects of the project. One of those could be a progress report designed for staff not involved in the day-to-day management of the project. This is the report which has as its primary purpose the provision of information. Its aim is to do no more than make people who are interested in what is happening aware of what is happening. The report is saying simply: 'Here is some information that we think you ought to know.'

    In preparing this kind of report, you should define the purpose of the report by asking these questions:

    -   How much detail should be included in the report?
    -   Is the information in the report cleared for general circulation?

- Who will receive the report?
- What value will the information be to the readers?
- At what level should the information be pitched?
- Is this a one-off report?
- Will the report be filed for reference or thrown away after reading?

2. *To provide a record.* The main purpose of this kind of report is to record information that may need to be accessed at some stage in the future. The minutes of a meeting is an example of a report whose purpose is partly to provide a record of information, which may include decisions taken. However, there are many other cases where a report is compiled solely for the purpose of recording information. Sometimes, such a report will be written only for the writer's own files. Alternatively, it might be circulated to other readers.

    Often, the purpose of a report 'for the record' is to provide a contemporaneous account of information collected or decisions taken. The report is always there as an *aide-memoire* should the writer or any other reader want to refer to it in the future. Should the subject of the report ever be raised again, the report stands as a (theoretically) incontestable record of what happened. If there is a dispute about facts or about action taken, the writer of the report can say: 'Look, this report was written at the time when the information was fresh in everybody's mind.'

    There is sometimes an element of self-preservation about reports written for the record, especially when they languish in the writer's own files. The report lies there as evidence that information was properly collected, opinions were properly considered, decisions were properly taken, should there be a dispute in the future. Not surprisingly, therefore, such reports are most common in public bodies, where decisions can become the subject of public debate and may have to be defended months or even years after they were taken. However, they are also to be found in commercial bodies.

Take, for example, a situation where a member of staff has been disciplined. The manager responsible for the disciplinary procedures will write a report at the end of the process detailing what was said and what was done. However, that report will not be circulated widely, although it may be sent to one or two other managers involved in the disciplinary process. It is written chiefly for the record – in case there should be any need to take further disciplinary action against the same individual in the future. Indeed, such a report has potentially important significance in any legal action that might arise from future disciplinary proceedings.

In writing any report for the record, you should ask these questions.

- Why is it important to record this information now?
- Who might want to refer to this information in the future?
- Why might people want to refer to this information in the future?
- Is the report likely to be used in any legal or quasi-legal proceedings?
- Does the wording of the report need to be approved by any other people?

3. *To answer a specific query.* A considerable number of reports are written in order to provide an answer to a specific question or request for information on a clearly defined topic. In these cases, the purpose of the report and the audience for it are clear to the

writer from the outset. In this kind of report, the 'terms of reference' are defined by the person who has asked for the report. (We shall be exploring the nature of terms of reference in more detail in the next chapter.) This is not to say, the terms of reference will make it easy for the report writer to research and compile the report.

The terms of reference of this kind of report could suggest a simple report or a lengthy and complex report. An example of a query demanding a comparatively simple report would be: 'Provide a report on the profitability over the past 12 months of our Birmingham branch.' Depending on the amount of detail requested, this would be a comparatively simple report to compile. A query demanding a much more complex report would be something like: 'Provide a report on the feasibility of opening a chain of branches for our company in the US.' In order to produce a report that satisfied this need, the writer would need to consider a large number of different issues. Whereas the first report might take only a couple of pages and not much more than an hour or two to compile, the second report could take a team of people weeks, even months, and might run to a hundred or more pages.

In writing a report to answer a single query, you should ask these questions:

- Is the query (the terms of reference) framed in a way that is clear and unambiguous?
- Is it clear what kind of report the recipient wants?
- What level of knowledge does the report's recipient have about the topic to be dealt with in the report?
- What use will the recipient make of the report?

7

- What is the deadline for delivering the report?

4. *To recommend a decision.* This is the kind of report which is produced when a board of directors, group of managers or people running a public body want some advice about how to approach a particular decision. Like the reports already mentioned, this kind of report involves collecting information. But the writer or writers (and any people who put their name to the report) will be expected to consider a range of options about the issue under consideration. The report writers will be judged on the quality of recommendations as much as on the comprehensiveness of the information contained in the report. Normally, people called on to produce this kind of report are experts in the subject matter (although this is not always the case).

Reports used to recommend decisions are used in both the public and private sector. Central government, for instance, often sets up bodies charged with compiling a report and making recommendations on various areas of public concern. A 'green paper' is a report produced by a government department that explores a range of options about a topic. By contrast, a 'white paper' says what the government plans to do. Reports that recommend decisions are also common in local government where an agenda item for a committee meeting will often be accompanied by a report from officers recommending a course of action to the committee.

Similarly, in the private sector, a manager or management committee may be charged with investigating a course of action and making recommendations either to the board of directors or other group of managers.

In writing a report to recommend a decision, you should ask these questions:

- What is the context of the recommendation the report will make?
- Will the report's recipients require one recommendation or a choice of options?
- Who should be involved in discussing the recommendation?
- What evidence will be needed to support the recommendation?
- In what timescale will the recommendation be needed?
- Have the effects of implementing the recommendation been fully considered?

5. *To influence opinion.* The purpose of this kind of report is to win over people to a particular point of view. Generally speaking, such a report will be produced for wide circulation. On rare occasions, such a report will be on sale in bookshops – for example, people queued for hours to be the first to buy the Denning Report, which investigated alleged government sex scandals in the 1960s. That, however, is a rare case. In most instances, this kind of report is produced by a voluntary organization or public sector body that wants to win opinion-formers to its point of view. However, in some cases an opinion-forming report is produced by a commercial organization or trade body that wants to put its point of view to a wider audience.

Because the purpose of the report is to influence opinions, the report writer has to pay great attention to the quality of research and the accuracy of the facts mentioned in the report, as obvious omissions or inaccurate facts will undermine the report's credibility. Opponents of the organization's point of view will be looking for ways to discredit the report.

Another important point is the quality of the argument. If the report aims to form opinions among a knowledgeable section of the community, the way the report writer constructs his case will be crucial. Readers will expect the argument to be connected together with logical links and supported with valid and illuminating examples. But people's opinions are also driven by their emotions, so subject matter and presentation which appeals to the heart as well as the head may also be effective.

The presentation of a report such as this will also be important. In most cases, readers will not be obliged to read the report as a manager would with a business report that landed on his desk. Instead, potential readers must be enticed into reading the report. Producing the report in an attractive and readable format is one way to encourage readership. Giving it an appealing, even provocative title, is another way.

If you have to write a report to influence people's opinions, you should consider these points:

- Which people is the report seeking to influence?
- What is their current opinion?
- Why are we seeking to change their opinions?
- What are our strongest arguments and how can they be put over most effectively?
- How should we deal with hostile points of view?
- What information should the report contain and at what level of detail?
- In what other ways can the report be made more influential?

6. *To gain publicity*. The purpose of this kind of report is to raise the profile of the organization that produces it. It can be similar to the previous kind of report (which can be used to generate publicity) but is

also different in some important respects. Several of the kinds of reports can be used to generate media coverage, but there is a category of report whose sole purpose is to produce publicity. Sometimes, this kind of report is produced when the organization finds it difficult to generate publicity in other ways. Often such a report contains the results of a survey.

Consider, for example, a company that wants to publicize some of the services it provides. Perhaps it sells life assurance policies. It conducts a survey of the different policies held by people and what they think of them. It asks questions about why people invest in life assurance policies and the value they believe they get from them. It probes a range of potentially controversial issues, such as what people think should be done to improve the service provided by life assurance companies. Then the results are presented with an interpretive commentary in a report. Providing the survey has been conducted in an authoritative way, some newspapers and magazines will regard the results of the survey in the report as a worthy news item.

If you are asked to produce a report in order to gain publicity, you should ask the following questions:

- Why do we wish to gain publicity for the subject of this report?
- How will the publicity help our organization?
- Will the report actually produce positive publicity or could there be negative spin-off?
- Is the content of the report genuinely newsworthy?
- Which kinds of news organizations are most likely to publicize the report?
- How can the presentation of the report make it more newsworthy?

7. *To meet a statutory obligation.* Many reports are produced because the law says they must be produced. For example, a company's annual report and accounts is produced to meet a statutory requirement. A significant proportion of the contents of an annual report are specified by law, although publicly quoted companies often include a considerable amount of other material in their annual reports. Many public bodies are also required to produce statutory reports. For example, local councils are obliged to submit a range of reports to different government departments.

    In producing a report of this kind, the writer must make certain that all the information specified by law is included in the report – and that the information is provided in the way decreed by the regulations. Clearly, this is a specialized task and the writers of such reports will generally be experts in their fields and familiar with the legal requirements.

    One problem that sometimes arises with statutory reports is how to include non-statutory information alongside that demanded by the law. In some cases, there is a clash of views between the person responsible for reporting the statutory information and others who might want to give the report a wider appeal. If this happens, it is important that the primary purpose of the report – to meet the statutory requirements – is fully met. There is no reason, however, why some such reports (for example, a company's annual report) should not also seek to achieve broader aims, but these must be carefully defined.

    If you are asked to produce a report to meet a statutory requirement, you should ask these questions:

- Have the statutory requirements of the report been checked with the primary source?
- Has the information been presented in the way required by the body receiving it?
- What other useful information could be included in the report?

A flexible business tool

From what we have seen so far, it is clear that the report is a flexible business tool. (Indeed, a tool that can be used by public sector and voluntary organizations as well.) One danger is that you might think of a report in too narrow a way. It is easy to see how this might happen. You will be familiar with receiving only a limited range of reports in the course of your own work. So your view of the role of the report will be coloured by the reports you receive. You need to adopt a wider view of how you can use different types of report to achieve your objectives.

In skilled hands, the report can be used to achieve many things.

To summarize:

- Understand the characteristics of a report.
- Define the exact purpose of the report you plan to draft.
- Consider the different roles of the report as a business tool.

2

GETTING STARTED

THE NATURE OF REPORT WRITING

Writing a report is like going on a journey in which there is a beginning and an end but several alternative routes in between. There is no one correct way to write a report because, as we saw in chapter one, there are so many different purposes that the report might have to satisfy. There are, however, a number of different processes that might be involved in writing a specific report. Which ones you use will depend on the exact nature of the report.

Reports fall into two main categories:

- Regular reports.
- One–off reports.

Before considering the processes used in report writing, we should first examine the characteristics of these two types of reports.

Regular reports

Regular reports provide the bulk of the filling for many managers' in-trays. They arrive monthly, weekly, even, in some cases, daily. Most regular reports provide historical performance-related information. For example, a financial report on the previous month, a sales report for the past week, a production report on yesterday's output of the factory. As such, these reports tend to contain mostly financial information, although they may also contain some text commentary on the figures and, indeed, present some of the figures in graphical formats.

If you are made responsible for producing a regular report such as this, you will inherit a set of processes for producing it. The sources of the information to be included in the report should already be clearly identified. The information should arrive according to an agreed timetable. It will be your job to take that information and present it in the report which you produce to an agreed format.

However, if you are asked to take on responsibility for producing a regular report (or if you have been producing one for some time) it might be worth asking a few fundamental questions about the report.

First, why was this report first produced? Many organizations have reports that have been produced for so long that people have forgotten why they were first wanted. The original purpose of the report is lost in the mists of time. If a regular report has been produced for any length of time – say, more than two years – it is at least worth asking whether the reason for producing the report still exists.

Secondly, does the report still serve any useful purpose? It is possible that the original reason for the report no longer exists, but that it is now used for other purposes. Alternatively, perhaps the report is no longer used at all. There are two ways to find out whether a particular report is still used. One is to ask managers if they still find it useful. Some managers may provide useful feedback, but other managers may not be entirely frank about their use of the report. Another way to test the value of a report is not to send it out or to delay its distribution by a week or two. If nobody rings to ask where it is, you have a good idea of its value.

Thirdly, could the report be changed to make it more useful? If managers are still using the report, but for reasons which have departed somewhat from the original purpose, it is possible that the report could be redesigned to serve the new purpose more effectively. You should ask the people who use the report whether all the information is still relevant, whether the information could be presented in new ways, what new information should be included, and whether the report should appear at the same frequency.

One-off reports

One-off reports are produced for a specific purpose (see chapter one for more detail on the possible purposes). If you are asked to produce a report such as this, it might seem that you are starting from scratch. In fact, that might not be the case. It is possible that your organization has produced a report on a similar topic, which might provide some guidance as to the approach you should adopt.

However, whether that is the case or not, the starting point is to obtain the terms of reference which should define your task. Many of the criticisms of inadequate reports arise because terms of reference were not adequately defined at the outset. So what makes good terms of reference? Consider the boss who says: 'Let me have a report on how the new product is doing.' What does he mean? If this statement is supposed to be his terms of reference for a report it is deficient in several important respects. In fact, this boss's request does not constitute proper terms of reference at all. Where does it fall short of what is needed?

First, it is not precise. Terms of reference should state exactly what is needed. The phrase 'how the new product is doing' could mean anything. Does it mean how the product is selling? Does it refer to the product's reliability? Does it deal with the product's marketing and distribution? It is not clear. Indeed, if there is more than one product, which product is the boss talking about?

Secondly, the boss's statement gives no indication of

why he needs the information. Does he need the information in order to plan a marketing campaign? Or to review the manufacturing capacity? Or review pricing strategy? Where a report is to be used for a specific purpose, the terms of reference should make clear what the purpose is.

Thirdly, the boss's statement gives no indication of what kind of report is wanted. Does he expect a couple of sheets of paper with basic summary information? Or does he want a 100-page bound briefing book, the result of considerable research? Neither does the statement give any indication of a timescale for the report. When does the manager want the report? Next week? Next month? Tomorrow?

It is vital – not optional – to have full and complete terms of reference before starting work on a report. In order to avoid any confusion, the terms of reference should always be in writing, and signed by the person requesting the report. No doubts, no comebacks. Ideally, terms of reference will include a precise and unambiguous statement of the purpose of the report, an indication of why the report is needed, the amount of detail required and a target date for the report's delivery. So, instead of his vague statement, the boss would have issued some terms of reference like this:

- Produce a report on the sales of the new vacuum cleaner in each of our sales regions. The report should:

  - show how sales are performing in comparison with the competition.
  - assess the impact of current marketing activities and make suggestions as to how marketing could be improved.
  - consider the likely impact of different pricing policies.

The report should be submitted in time to be considered by members of the marketing sub-committee at its meeting on 20 August.

What should you do if you receive terms of reference which are not as complete as this? The answer is to approach the person requesting the report and ask for more precise terms of reference. Make the approach in writing – probably by memo – as a question in writing usually elicits a response in writing. And, as Samuel Goldwyn might have said, a verbal instruction is not worth the paper it's written on.

REVIEWING THE SITUATION

You have precise terms of reference for a one-off report. What next? You need to consider how you will set about producing the report. In doing this you will need to consider a number of issues including whether you will produce the report alone or as part of a team or working party, what resources you will need in order to produce the report and how you will schedule the work during the time you have to produce the report. We must consider each of these issues in turn.

Alone or together?

The first major issue to consider is whether you will produce the report by yourself or as part of a team. In many cases, that question will effectively be answered for you. If the request is for a report of modest scope based on information on which you are the acknowledged master, clearly you will produce the report yourself. On the other hand, the organization wanting the report may have established a working party or study group and given it terms of reference to produce a report. This approach is common in the public sector with central and local government bodies, but it is also used occasionally in the private sector.

There is a middle group of cases where you need to

decide whether you should produce a report by yourself or form your own working party to do it. Which issues will help you take the best decision?

First, you need to consider the scope of the information that must be collected for the report. Can you reasonably get all the information yourself? Is some of the information outside your own area of expertise or so specialized it needs an expert? Does some of the information have to be collected from other parts of the country or abroad? If the scope of the information you need for the report is wide, then you should seriously consider forming a working party.

Secondly, you need to consider whether the report involves considering significant policy issues. Are they issues that you feel confident taking decisions about alone? Or would the views of other people be welcome? Indeed, are the views of others essential in order to give credibility to the final report? Are there specialist areas which need to be reviewed by someone with technical expertise?

If you decide that other people need to be involved in helping you to produce the report, there are two main ways in which you can involve them.

1. *You can work with them in a bilateral way.* That is you divide up the work needed to produce the report into sections. Then you assign each block of work to a different individual. You manage and coordinate the whole project and probably write the finished report from drafts on different sections compiled by the people working on them. If you adopt this approach, you need to consider the following points:

    • You must make sure everybody working on

the project is aware of the total scope of the project. They should understand how their piece of the jigsaw fits into the whole.

- You should thoroughly brief each individual working on the report on what is expected of him. He should understand what information he is expected to produce, how much detail will be needed, how his information will be used, and the timescale he must work in.

- After each individual has produced his contribution to the report, you should set aside time to discuss it with him. You must make sure you thoroughly understand all the information each person has provided before you issue the final draft of the report. You should ask each person to check for accuracy that part of the report to which he has contributed.

2. *You can set up a working party.* If you adopt this approach you will assemble a group of people to work together in a more formal way in compiling and writing the report. In forming a working party, you need to make sure it is small enough to work effectively but large enough to include all the expertise you need. However, it is not essential to have everybody working on the report as a member of the working party. You can have a core of people on the working party calling, as needed, on the expertise of outside specialists. But in forming the working party you must ensure that its membership will endow the finished report with the credibility and authority that is needed. This means that every person on the working party should be chosen because he is able to make a measurably effective contribution to the final report.

As the person originally charged with producing the report, you will chair the working party and take ultimate responsibility for the finished report.

The working party should only meet in order to progress the work on the project. You should not allow working party meetings to turn into talking shops. This means that each meeting should have a clear aim and agenda. For example, the first meeting will scope the project, identify the work that needs to be completed, set a timetable for each stage of the project and assign responsibility for different parts of the work to specific individuals.

If the report is produced by a working party, there are several other issues that you need to manage. These include how differences of opinion between members of the working party are resolved and how the report is written. These are dealt with in later chapters.

Finding the resources

The next issue you need to consider even before you embark on researching and writing your report is the resources you need to complete the task to a satisfactory standard. For the very simplest of reports, those resources may consist of little more than a writing pad and pen, and a few hours of your own time. But, in reality, a report does not need to become too complex before it requires a significant amount of resources. In producing reports, the use of resources becomes an important issue when you need money, staff time and (possibly) office equipment above and beyond those that you use in your daily work as a matter of course. For example, you may have responsibility for producing a range of regular reports. You will already have the staffing and other resources necessary to do that.

It is when a large project comes along – probably, what we have classified as a 'one-off' report – that you need to consider the use of resources more carefully. At a simple level, you can consider the resources you need under three headings – staff time, external resources and general expenses.

- *Staff time.* Producing a report of any significant size is likely to use up considerable amounts of staff time – time which will be diverted from other work. You need to make a judgement about whether you can absorb the amount of time needed in your department's general work, or whether you need a budget for extra staff time. It can be useful to make a rough calculation of the number of days each member of staff is likely to be working on the report. Multiply the number of days by the daily employment cost (salary plus national insurance and other employment expenses, such as office space) to produce an estimate of the cost of staff time needed to produce the report. Then ask the question: does this report justify this expenditure? If you are not sure that it does, it might be worth showing the costs to the manager who has commissioned the report. Perhaps the expense of the report will give him second thoughts or get him to revise his views of the task.

- *External resources.* In the case of a large report, you might need to use different external resources. For example, you may need to engage the services of consultants with special expertise to help you research and compile either parts of the report or the whole report. Typically consultants might be needed for tasks such as:

  - Providing technical expertise – for example engineering, financial or legal.
  - Conducting surveys – for example, market research or focus group interviews.
  - Producing artwork – for example, charts, graphs, maps or special drawings.

Before you begin work on the report, you should assess what external resources are needed and make arrangements to engage them. You should provide a detailed briefing to all external people working on the report. It is also essential to define the work you expect them to do and the timetable in which they should perform it in a written contract, which in simple cases can be a commissioning letter.

- *General expenses.* Again, the level of general expenses can vary dramatically depending on the nature of the report. For a small report, the general expenses are not likely to be much more than the cost of printing and distribution. For larger reports, you could incur a considerable range of general expenses. Categories to consider when drawing up your budget are:

  - Report publishing. Can you or your staff complete the work or will you need the help of a desktop publishing bureau?
  - Report printing. How large will the report be? How many copies will be needed? What sort of binding will be used? (Chapter six provides more guidance on this issue.)
  - Travelling expenses. Will you or others working on the report need to travel to collect information for it?
  - Working party costs. If there is a working party, what about the travelling expenses of members attending meetings as well as the cost of rooms for meetings?
  - Market research/surveys. If you are commissioning these, have the costs been included in the budget?
  - Library subscriptions. If the research involves access to specialized libraries, have these costs been included?

- Artwork. Will you need to commission an artist to prepare artwork for charts or drawings and so on or for the front cover?
- General overheads. Are there any other general costs which ought to be included in the budget?

How sophisticated you make the budgeting exercise depends on the size and complexity of the report. For a very small report, there is probably not much point in drawing up a budget. For a medium sized report, a brief note of the main costs should be enough. For a large project, conducted over several weeks or months, you might want to create formal processes in order to build a budget and subsequently to monitor actual costs against that budget. It is worth pointing out that the costs of a large report, involving the work of several senior managers over a period of weeks, could run into several tens of thousands of pounds.

There is another value from the budgeting exercise. Just as there is no free lunch, so there is no free report. If more managers are aware of the costs of producing reports, it will enable them to gain a better grasp of the trade-off between the costs of creating them and the value they provide.

Scheduling the work
In nine cases out of ten – and probably even more often – a report is needed by a specific date. That date may be tomorrow in the case of a small report. It may be in a year's time – even two years time – in the case of a major project. Where you are faced with producing a report for which the amount of work is clear and the subject matter is familiar, you will probably not need to draw up a formal schedule. The way you will handle the work will form up automatically in your mind ('I'll look up the facts on Tuesday, write it on Wednesday, and get it typed and printed on Thursday').

But for larger reports, this informal approach is unlikely to be adequate either for scoping the project to start with or monitoring its progress as you proceed. This is especially true when the production of the report involves several people and the use of outside resources. In scoping a project, you need to perform three basic tasks, which will vary in complexity depending on the size of the project:

1. List all the different tasks that must be completed in order to produce the report. Each task should involve a self-contained element of the work such as completing interviews, conducting a survey, writing the final draft of the report or printing the report. You should estimate the amount of time needed to complete each task in hours or days and also the elapse time – the length of the period over which those hours or days will be used. For example, a task might take eight days spread over four weeks.
2. Place the tasks on a critical path. You and your team must complete the tasks in a logical order. List the tasks in the order in which you must complete them. You can do this diagrammatically, showing where one task must be completed before another starts and where one task overlaps another.
3. Finally, allocate each task to a specific person or team of people. In some cases, you might be allocating a task to an outside consultant or specialist supplier. In such cases, you will need to liaise with the specialist to discover how much time he believes he will need to complete the task.

At the end of this process, you should have a written work plan which shows all the tasks in critical path order with start and finish dates and with responsibilities allocated. This will be an important working document as the project proceeds, for it will enable you to keep control of the different tasks. You should regularly monitor the progress of the project against the dates in the work plan.

To summarize:

- Understand the difference between regular and one-off reports.
- Decide whether to produce your report by yourself or as a member of a team.
- Estimate the resources you need to produce the report.
- Schedule the work needed to complete the task.

3

RESEARCHING A REPORT

RESEARCH WITH PURPOSE

Every report has a purpose. That much we discovered in chapter one. The skilled researcher directs his research in a way that uncovers the information he needs in order to make his report serve the purpose for which it is intended. This point is important because too many report writers veer to one of two extremes.

One type loves research and immerses himself in it with enthusiasm. Unfortunately, he follows every little byway in the research material he finds with the result that he amasses a huge body of information. Too much to produce a well directed report. The other type finds research a bit of a bore. He skates over the most important points and assumes he knows the rest. As a result, he thinks he knows it all (when he doesn't) and is in danger of drawing the wrong conclusions.

If you are a skilled researcher, you will position yourself somewhere between these two extremes. You will direct your research so that you produce material that serves the purpose of the report. You will not become bogged down in unneeded minutiae but you will make sure that you obtain the detail you require to make a convincing case.

Which brings us to another important point about research. Bluntly, is the purpose of your report to relay facts, to discover something previously unknown or to put a point of view? All three will influence the way you approach the research. If you are relaying facts, the main focus of your concern is to find the relevant facts and confirm their accuracy. If you are seeking to discover something previously unknown, you may need to spend quite a lot of time trawling through literature looking for information that is relevant to the subject you are researching. If you are arguing a case, you will not be seeking information in an impartial way, but be looking for evidence that supports your case.

All this boils down to a simple point. When people compile a report there is often a 'hidden agenda' – an under-cover purpose to the report – not stated in the formal terms of reference. If there is a hidden agenda for your report, you need to understand what it is and direct your research to fulfil it.

Freshening a regular report

Much of what is said above applies to all reports, but perhaps chiefly to the kinds of reports we have termed 'one-offs'. As we have seen, a large number of reports are regular, produced with the same categories of information and in the same format on every reporting cycle. On the face of it, research does not play too large a part in these reports. The information comes in from the same sources every reporting period and is massaged into the chosen format of the report.

In fact, even this kind of regular report needs a new research initiative every once in a while. To begin with, such reports become stale. The format chosen, which originally served a useful purpose, becomes out of date. Yet through inertia, it never gets changed. Another problem is that the quality of the information declines. People whose task it is to provide information for regular reports soon learn when they can get away with errors, inaccuracies or inconsistencies. As they creep up this unwelcome learning curve, the value of the information they submit slips down a quality slide.

There are several courses of action you can take with regular reports to make sure they remain useful. First, you should periodically ask the users of the report for their opinion on the report's value. What information in it do they find especially helpful? Which information do they scarcely look at? What do they use the information for? Is there any information not regularly included in the report which they would welcome?

Secondly, you should periodically audit the accuracy and completeness of the raw material information you use in compiling the report. Go back to source and check the accuracy of the information against the primary sources from which it was compiled. Question the compilers of the information about the methodologies they use. This could uncover fundamental flaws in both the nature and quality of information they are submitting.

Finally, examine the way in which you compile the report. Are you presenting the information in the most helpful format? Is the information presented in a way that helps the managers use it to take decisions? Does the report need more or less detail?

It is by adopting this constantly critical approach, rather than just accepting what is there, that a regular report remains a valuable working document rather than another pile of bumph in the in-tray.

SOURCES OF INFORMATION

The next point to consider is where you will obtain the information you need for your report. With a regular report, this is unlikely to be too much of a problem because (as we have seen) the sources of information are already defined. However, it could be a problem with a one-off report, especially if the report is complex or you are not especially familiar with the subject matter.

Suppose, for example, you are commissioned to produce a report which examines the feasibility of your company moving into a new line of business. By definition, this is a subject about which you will not know much, if anything. It is not like producing a report on, say, the past year's performance of your own department where you are already familiar with much of the information and know where to find the rest of it. Instead, you are moving into uncharted seas. How do you set about the research?

With this, or any other research project, the sources of information you can tap fall into two main categories – those within your organization and those outside it. We shall consider both in turn.

Internal sources of information

Your own organization is a vast reservoir of information, perhaps a greater information resource than you realize. In a large organization, you will probably be aware of only a fraction of the main information resources in your company – for example, the databases that can be accessed on your computer, the books in the company library, the body of reports and research produced over the years. Beyond your own knowledge lie great oceans of information. In fact, the breadth and depth of information in your organization is probably much greater than you imagine. We need to consider the potential information sources you can access under a number of headings.

- *People.* This is the primary source of information in your company, arguably the most valuable and almost certainly the most under exploited. Every member of staff is a potential mine of information, not only about his current job responsibilities, but about his previous work experiences. Take the case of researching a new business area. Perhaps there are members of staff who worked in that area in the past and have useful information to provide or who can, at least, point you in the right direction for your research.

The problem is how to find out which members of staff know what, especially if you work in a large organization with hundreds or thousands of employees. Your first port of call should be the personnel department. It should retain the CVs of all members of staff who applied for jobs. It may have other records about the specific expertise of employees, such as those who have attended training courses or conferences. Finding those staff members with the knowledge you are looking for could be a lengthy experience, unless the personnel records are computerized and can be searched using keywords. Alternatively, you could put out a call for people with the knowledge you want through a company newsletter, information bulletin or noticeboard.

In drawing on the knowledge of in-house people, you need to keep a couple of points in mind. First, how recent is their experience? If they have not had any direct contact with their subject for several years, they may be out of touch. Their information and views could be positively misleading rather than helpful. Secondly, at what level were they involved with the subject you are researching? It may be that they were only involved at a junior level but you need a more senior viewpoint. Finally, what opinions do they hold about the subject? You must take care to treat their opinions with caution. They represent only one point of view and there may be other more relevant views to take into account.

- *Company library.* This is an obvious source of information, but only the largest organizations have their own company library. A professional company librarian is familiar not only with research materials in his collection but with other sources of information. He will be able to provide considerable advice on seeking out published sources of information.

If your organization does not have its own library, it certainly has what you might call informal mini-libraries scattered around the offices. Individual managers have collected books over the years. It is worth contacting some of them to see if they have anything that might be relevant to your research or if they know of any relevant publications.

- *Databases.* Increasingly, large amounts of information are stored on computers. In the past, most of the information was numerical but increasingly larger amounts of text are stored on databases. You should find out what databases are available in your organization and decide whether any of them hold information that could be relevant to your research.

External sources of information
Outside your organization lie thousands of organizations holding information that could be relevant to a particular research report. Some of the most important categories of organization are:

- *Public libraries.* There has been a revolution in many public libraries in the past decade. No longer are they just dusty repositories for ageing detective stories. Instead, many have built substantial business collections, both in the borrowing and reference sections. Some libraries even offer specialized services, such as copies of company annual reports. The local librarian is helpful and will tell you what research sources are available in his own and nearby libraries.

- *Customers and suppliers.* Both these groups are potential useful sources of information which are frequently overlooked. Of their very nature, both have a wide experience of dealing with different kinds of organizations. In certain circumstances, your contacts within customers or suppliers may be willing to help with information or with tips about where to seek the facts you need.

- *Trade associations.* Most companies and public sector bodies belong to at least one trade association or similar kind of organization. Such bodies exist partially to be a repository of information about their relevant area. Many maintain their own libraries. Membership frequently provides access to the library. Even if your company is not a member of the association you believe might be able to help in your research, it is still possible you could access its information. Some associations allow outside researchers to use their libraries for a fee. Alternatively, the association's public affairs officer might be willing to help with limited advice to get you started.

- *Professional associations.* As with trade associations, many managers in your organization will belong to their relevant professional association. Again, the same principles apply. You can seek access to the library of the relevant professional association.

- *Online databases.* In the past few years, a new type of company – the professional information provider – has appeared. These build huge databases of both numerical and textual information. For a subscription fee and connection charge, you can access these databases from a PC or workstation in your own office. Although not cheap, online databases provide an increasingly important information resource, not least because a large number of them already offer 'full text retrieval' of important business journals such as the *Financial Times*. Using specially written software, it is possible to conduct keyword searches on huge amounts of text to find items that are relevant.

- *Conferences and exhibitions.* Most trades and industries have regular conferences and exhibitions which cater for their needs. Attending these can prove a useful source of information. However, you gain the most benefit from an exhibition – especially some of the larger trade shows – if you attend with a clear information-gathering purpose in mind. Most big shows produce good catalogues which provide a guide to the exhibition as well as a useful source of reference afterwards.

RESEARCH TECHNIQUES

At the same time as you are identifying the sources of information you will use in compiling your report, you also need to give some thought to the research techniques you will use. Some of the most common techniques are:

- *Desk research.* This term refers to the systematic sifting of information already published in books, magazines, newspapers and other documents. It is often the essential first step to a research project for it helps to identify the main issues which are important, define the boundaries of the research and uncover sources of further information. As a first phase, desk research also helps you to understand more fully the topic you are researching before you move on to other phases of research, such as interviews or surveys.

If you have not done much desk research before, it

might at first seem rather daunting. Where do you start? These tips should help:

– Seek the help of a good librarian in identifying main sources of information about your subject.
– As you identify books that are possibly useful, use the contents and the index to narrow down those which are likely to be of most help.
– As a first step, skim-read material, in order to gain an indication of its relevance. Do not waste time ploughing through long texts of only marginal importance.
– Study the most relevant texts more closely, making notes on or photocopying those sections of particular importance.
– When researching from newspapers and magazines, concentrate initial research on those periodicals that provide a regular index – for example *The Times* and *The Economist*.
– In unindexed periodicals, look for regular topic sections that appear in every issue – for example 'new orders', 'company news' – that might contain information of relevance rather than ploughing through the whole of every issue.
– Treat desk research as a voyage of discovery rather than a tedious job to complete in the minimum possible time. For example, look closely at the references in relevant books. The referenced works might provide more valuable information than the book you are studying.

● *Interviews.* You could find that you need to obtain information by interview from people in your own organization or outside it. You can conduct interviews either face to face or over the telephone. In general, telephone interviews work best when you already know the interviewee and the interview is reasonably short – say, less than half an hour.

Beyond that length, telephone interviews tend to become trying and increasingly unproductive. However, there are isolated instances when you might want to conduct a longer interview. One case would be if the person you are interviewing is overseas.

For the longer, more complex interview you should always opt for the face to face approach because it is more likely to provide you with insights and detail you may well have missed in a phone interview. In order to get the best from interviewing, you should follow these tips:

– Always understand the purpose of the interview. Be quite clear in your own mind why you want to interview a specific individual and the kind of information you hope to gain from him.
– Brief the interviewee on the purpose of the interview at least a couple of days before it takes place. Preferably, you should brief the interviewee in writing. This will give him time to prepare and assemble any background information he needs before you arrive.
– Prepare a written list of the areas you want to discuss before you go into the interview. This will help you think through the structure you want the interview to take. In some cases, you may actually want to ask a list of specific questions. In others, you might want to talk around specific topics in a more general way.
– Take the interview at a measured pace. Give the interviewee time to catch his breath by engaging in a few pleasantries before you plunge into the formal part of the interview. Move at a business-like pace through the topics you want to cover, but make sure you give your interviewee as much time as he needs to answer each question. Otherwise, you may miss useful detail.

– Decide before you start the interview, whether you are going to make notes or tape-record it. Check with your interviewee that he is happy with whichever option you choose.

– Thank your interviewee for his help at the end of the interview (and it does no harm to send a thank-you letter afterwards if he has been especially helpful). Ask if you can contact him again briefly by phone to check any points that need further clarification.

● *Questionnaires and surveys.* These are an effective means of assembling data when you want to collect information from a fairly large number of people in a structured way. Questionnaires can be useful either to produce factual information (for example, which makes of office equipment do you use?) or opinions (for example, what do you think of different makes of office equipment?). You can conduct questionnaires and surveys by post, telephone or face to face interviews or a combination. The method you choose depends on how many people you want to contact, the nature of the questions, and the amount of detail you require in the replies.

The following tips should help when organizing a questionnaire or survey:

– Decide on the purpose of the questionnaire. What information are you trying to discover? What use will you put the information to in your report? Is there a better way of obtaining the information you want?

– Decide on the most effective way of conducting the questionnaire – by post, telephone or face to face interviews. Then draw up the questions. Be realistic about both the number of questions you can expect people to answer and the topics they will be prepared to provide information about. Consider offering a small incentive for completing the questionnaire – such as a summary of the findings.

– If using a postal questionnaire, make the printed form easy to complete and return. Include a postage-paid envelope. Include a short and personalized letter asking the recipient to complete the questionnaire. In the letter, explain why you are conducting the questionnaire. Target questionnaire recipients carefully. Only send questionnaire forms to relevant people. Give a deadline for returning questionnaires.

– If possible, test the draft questionnaire on a small sample of people similar to those who will receive the final version. Use the results of the pilot testing to refocus questions and smooth out ambiguities.

● *Observation and recording.* This category of research covers a spectrum of different activities. At one end is a complex scientific experiment or testing programme, such as that carried out on a new drug by a pharmaceutical company. At the other, is the simple counting of information from a single source – such as counting the number of passengers who get on each train at a railway station.

At the top end of the range, a major experimentation programme requires enormous amounts of specialized expertise. However, there are more modest circumstances in which you could be called on to conduct some observation or recording in order to produce information for a report. The following tips should help:

– Understand clearly why you need the information for the report. What role will it play? Do you need information to support a particular point of view? How will the information be presented in the report and at what level of detail?

– Study the feasibility of collecting the information you need. Can the information be collected at a reasonable cost? Is it physically possible to collect the information and over what period of time will you need to deploy the resources?

– Devise the most effective way of collecting information. Will you need to collect information on a tally sheet? Is there any way you can use technology to collect the information more effectively? Test the method you propose to use before you move into the full programme in order to identify any problems.

To summarize:

- Conduct research with your report's ultimate purpose in mind.
- Consider ways to reinvigorate a regular report.
- Identify the sources of internal and external information you can access in research.
- Choose the research technique most appropriate to the task.

4

DRAWING THE RIGHT CONCLUSIONS

GETTING ORGANIZED

As the research for your report proceeds you will accumulate a mass of research material. You need to impose some order on this material rather than allowing it to develop into a muddle. One key to this is the careful filing and cross-referencing of research materials. How complex your filing system is, and how much cross-referencing you decide to do, depends on the size of your project. In a small project, the material you accumulate might well be organized successfully in two or three files, possibly even one. For larger projects a more complex filing system is needed.

You should give some thought to the filing system you will use at the outset of your research. But do not set the filing system in concrete at that stage. Be prepared to change the filing system as your research proceeds to accommodate the nature of the information you are accumulating.

There is no one correct way to organize a filing system for a report research project. But you should consider two possibilities. The first is to organize your research materials by document type. For example, you would create separate files for interview notes, survey results, press cuttings, other companies' literature and so on. Obviously, the exact files you create depend on the nature of the documents in your project. The benefit of this approach is that all documents of one type are in the same place. The drawback is that each document might contain information about several different topics.

The second approach is to create files for separate

topics. For example, you would create files for product specifications, advertising campaigns, sales force, branch offices and so on. Again, the exact nature of the files clearly depends on your project. The benefit of this approach is that all the information about each subject is in the same file. The drawback is that a document may also contain other information as well so that there is much irrelevant information in each file. And if a document contains information on more than one topic you have to photocopy it and place it in two or more files, so you multiply the amount of paper you are handling.

One way to overcome the drawbacks of both filing approaches, and to gain a firmer grip on your research material, is to cross-reference it as you gather it. Depending on your predilection, you can do this using a simple card file or a computer. Using a computer may involve learning a special piece of database or indexing software. So the software option is only worth pursuing for large projects – unless you already own and know how to use the software.

If you adopt the first approach – filing documents by document type – you give each file a title (for example, interview notes) and number each document in it sequentially starting at one. Then you can build up a topic reference card for each topic by noting topics and referencing to the file and document number. For example, suppose you are developing a report on marketing in Europe, you could develop topic cards for each European country in your report. Each entry on the card should give brief details (not more than 10 words) about the nature of the information to be found in the referenced document. For example, an entry might read: 'France: government sales statistics quoted in FT article – press cuttings file, document number 17.'

In any sizeable research project you should not underestimate the value of adopting this approach. Not only will you find it easier to access your research materials when you come to write your report, but the act of cross-referencing them will give you a much better understanding of the subject.

Sifting the evidence

If the report you are preparing is a medium or large one, you will soon realize, as you continue your research, that you are building a range of different kinds of information. You could have statistics, interview notes, press cuttings, extracts from books and reports, completed questionnaires and survey forms, comments from members of the public, submissions from fellow managers or outside bodies and so on and so on. Out of this disparate material you must construct your report. Where do you begin?

The starting point is to sift information that is relevant from that which is irrelevant or unimportant. The cross-referencing exercise described above will help you do this. Next you need to decide, from the relevant material, what is important and what less so. Not all the information has the same weight.

At this point, you should clearly have in mind the purpose of your report. This purpose is the lodestar which will guide you to the material of special value. As you study the material, you will find you are faced with a mass of facts and opinions. Looking at the facts, you should ask yourself: which are the facts that really matter? Are there certain key facts that clearly stand out as more important than others? Are the sources you consulted agreed about the facts? Are there surprising facts which were not expected and which might change your views?

Studying the opinions is also important. Not all

opinions carry the same weight. You need to evaluate the opinions expressed by the sources you consulted in a critical way. Do some opinions carry more weight than others because they derive from greater knowledge or experience of the subject? Are some opinions coloured by self-interest? Do people's opinions on particular topics generally agree or disagree? Are there any unexpected opinions which ought to be considered more carefully? Do the opinions change your view about the purpose of the report? These questions give just a flavour of the way in which you should approach the opinions you have been given.

As you consider and evaluate the facts and opinions you have gathered, you also need to think what you are going to do with the information. What you do will be largely determined by the purpose of your report. In chapter one, we defined seven main purposes for a report. If the purpose of your report is to provide information, you will summarize the facts and opinions in a logical sequence. If the purpose is to provide a record, you will summarize the main points together with any action taken on them, as a source of reference to be used in the future. If the purpose is to answer a specific query, you will provide as much information as is needed to answer that query fully so that the reader should not need to ask for any further information.

If the purpose of your report is to recommend a decision or decisions your task is rather more complex. You need to formulate your recommendations first. Then you will marshall the facts and opinions you need to justify the recommendations you have made. Similarly, if the purpose of your report is to influence opinion, you must decide on the conclusions you reach before you draft your report. Then you marshall the facts and opinions to lead up logically to those conclusions. If the purpose of your report is to gain publicity, you must decide which aspects you most wish to see publicized. Then you must make those the centre-piece of your report and build the other facts and opinions around them. If the purpose of your report is to meet a statutory obligation, you must make sure that you have included information to meet all the requirements laid down by the body to which you will submit it.

In every case, have the purpose of the report always at the front of your mind. And throughout the process of sifting your research, ask yourself: which is the material that best helps me achieve the report's purpose? (There is advice about writing the report in the next chapter.)

Sound arguments

If you are drafting the kind of report that is putting a point of view or making recommendations, you want people to agree with your conclusions. In achieving this, you need to bear three points in mind.

First, make sure that recommendations and conclusions are fully supported by the evidence in your report. Does the evidence you have provided really support the recommendation? Are there any logical flaws in your arguments? Is the evidence you have provided to support your recommendations complete and up to date? Does your recommendation go further than the evidence warrants? If you quoted expert opinions to support your recommendations are there expert opinions that could be quoted against them? If you used examples to support your argument are they typical?

Secondly, make sure that all the evidence you provide to support your conclusions or recommendations is completely accurate. Opponents of your views will search for flaws in your report in order to undermine it. They will seize on inaccuracies or half-truths with glee. Have you checked all the facts you quote with the primary source? (If you gleaned the fact from a second-ary source, it might be wrong.) As your argument progresses, is each point supported by accurate facts? Have you, by accident or design, left out any facts that clearly undermine your recommendations or conclusions? (Perhaps you should include them and explain why you still arrived at your conclusion.)

Thirdly, have in mind the outer-most boundaries of acceptable recommendations or conclusions to the readers of the report. In other words, keep your feet on the ground. You may think that the evidence in your report indicates that the company's product has no future and that, therefore, the company should go into liquidation, but this is unlikely to commend itself to the board of directors if it expected a report on future product strategy. You need to ask yourself a number of questions. What range of recommendations would be acceptable to the recipients of this report? Do their views rule out of bounds any particular recommendations? Will they be more predisposed to certain recommendations than others? All this does not mean that you should only present recommendations that your bosses will find immediately pleasing and acceptable, but that you should have a healthy awareness of the opinions and political forces at work in your organization.

WORKING WITH A TEAM

You may find yourself producing a report as part of a working party or team. Although this might be the only way of producing a large report, it raises other issues which you need to consider. For example, you need to agree with other members of your working party how the report will be compiled and the recommendations decided.

It helps if the working party has a clear idea about the purpose of the report right from the outset. The working party needs to understand what its recommendations must seek to achieve. For example, if the working party is set up by the district council to consider the provision of leisure facilities in Anytown, it needs to understand the constraints on any possible recommendations, such as the money that can be spent and the staff available to implement the recommendations. There is no point suggesting the building of an Olympic sports centre if the budget will only run to a kiddies' playground in the park. If all members of the working party understand the constraints on their recommendations, whole swathes of possible disagreements are removed right from the start.

The next point is to make sure that all members of the working party keep in touch with the general direction of the research as the project proceeds. This is especially important if members of the team are working on different parts of the research. You should make sure that the working party meets regularly to review the progress of each member's research area. Each member of the working party should be invited to explain the progress he has made and the significance he attaches to his findings. Then you should invite the working party to discuss those findings briefly. In this way, the working party starts to acquire a kind of collective understanding of the information as its work progresses. If this process runs smoothly, you should find that as the project nears its completion, most working party members are coming at the recommendations 'from the same direction'.

Inevitably, however, disagreements will arise. How should these be reconciled? The starting point is to understand the basis of each person's point of view. If you can show that the factual basis of one person's point of view is at fault, then the reason for the disagreement may disappear. But not all disagreements are like that. Fundamentally, disagreements arise because people view matters from a unique perception based on their own experience and understanding of what is significant and valuable. You cannot hope to change this kind of life-view that each person has. Nor should you. It is the reason why each person's opinion is valuable even if you disagree with it.

At the end of the day, disagreements in a working party about recommendations for a report can be settled in one of four ways:

1. *By a majority vote.* Strength: seen to be democratic. Weakness: not every choice has equal weight. Some know more about the topic than others.
2. *By accepting the decision of the chairman.* Strength: provides an outcome that the chairman can defend when the report goes public. Weakness: may leave a substantial body of dissatisfied working party members.
3. *By accepting the decision of the individual responsible for compiling that part of the report.* Strength: provides an expert view. Weakness: not all expert views are wise or sensible.
4. *By a compromise.* Strength: a compromise may satisfy everybody. Weakness: a compromise may dissatisfy everybody.

To summarize:

- Organize an effective filing and cross-reference system for research materials.
- Take account of the factors that bear on the recommendations you can realistically make.
- Establish procedures to encourage team members to work together effectively.

5

WRITING TO INFORM AND CONVINCE

A REPORT DISSECTED

When you pick up a report, you expect a document which is structured in a particular way and written in a clear style. As we have seen, a report should have a clear purpose. Giving a report its structure helps you to achieve that purpose by making the information in the report more accessible to the readers. There is no one structure that is suitable for all reports because reports differ greatly in length and complexity. However, you can structure any report around several common elements. These are:

- *Title page.* The title page is like that in a book. It contains the title of the report, its author, the date the report was published and the body that published it. What kind of title should you give your report? That depends on its purpose. If the purpose is to provide information, a record, answer a specific query or recommend a decision, you should choose a descriptive and functional title. For example, *New Office Block: recommendations for decoration and fitting out.* Note how this title contains the main gist of the report in the first three words followed by a phrase amplifying the exact purpose of the report after the colon. This is an effective style for many report titles.

  If the purpose of the report is to influence opinion or gain publicity, you might want to choose a more imaginative title designed to catch attention from people who don't have to read it. For example, the Prince of Wales' Business Leaders' Forum adopted this two tier approach for a report about company ethics:

Corporate Reputation in Tomorrow's Marketplace
A survey of the opinions and expectations of the young business leaders of today and tomorrow.

The two tier approach works well because it enables you to compose an attention-grabbing main title in not more than half a dozen words and then amplify it with a longer explanatory phrase underneath. In this case both are designed to attract the attention of those the report wants to influence.

You can use the same approach for reports designed to gain publicity. For example:

The European Lunchtime Report
A comparison of working lunchtime habits in Europe.

Published by a leading catering company, it surveyed the different lunchtime habits and favoured dishes across the continent in a way designed to make a good story for journalists.

- *Contents.* The contents page comes after the title page and provides a chronological list of the chapters or sections in the report and the page number on which each begins. In the shortest of reports, you might want to omit a contents page. In longer reports, you need to decide how much detail to put on the contents page. For example, do you want to list only the main sections of the report or subsections as well? As a general rule, listing sections only is sufficient for a medium-sized report. Include sub-sections in a longer report.

- *Terms of reference.* The next section to include is the

terms of reference of the report. This should be formally stated, often as it was given to you, as a means of showing readers the basis on which you approached the task. If the report was compiled by a working party or committee, you will also list the members and their job functions/titles after the terms of reference. In some cases, you may wish to include this information as part of the introduction (see below) rather than as a separate section.

• *Summary*. All but the very shortest of reports need a summary at the start. The summary has two purposes. The first is as a reference for the reader who has the time to read nothing but the summary. The second is to over-view the report for the reader who plans to study it in detail. The summary gives him a high-level view of the whole report before he starts to consider each section in turn. The length of the summary will be relative to the length of the report. For a short report, the summary might occupy no more than three or four paragraphs. For a long report, the summary might take up three or four pages.

Plainly, you should not write the summary until you have written the rest of the report. Even so, summary writing is difficult. What should you put in and what should you leave out? In general, the summary should describe the main topic areas that the report deals with, often from the point of view of the conclusion you reached about that topic. For example, suppose you have compiled a report about the feasibility of moving your company to a new office block. Your report will have a section dealing with how each department will move in phased programme from its existing accommodation to the new quarters. Such a section could run for a score or more pages, but the summary should be something like:

- The company should adopt a phased programme so that each department moves in successive weeks in the order accounts, marketing, central services and despatch.

This probably summarizes everything you need to say about this section of the report, although the detail of how the departments will move and why they should move in that order will be contained in the main body of the report.

- *Introduction.* The purpose of the introduction is to describe how you set about your task. You tell the report's reader how you interpreted your terms of reference and how you set about researching the subject matter for your report. You reveal briefly what is to follow, and perhaps you explain why you have placed the information in the order you have chosen. You do not need to embark on the meat of your evidence or your findings in the introduction. Indeed, you do best to keep your introduction as brief as possible. This section is often the best place to put information about the report's terms of reference and working party membership. You may also wish to use the introduction to acknowledge and thank any people who have helped you especially in providing information for the report.

- *Evidence and findings.* You now move into the main body of your report, where you start to present evidence and findings. How you do this depends on the nature of the information in your report. But you should consider a few general principles. First, does your information fall into a naturally logical order? Often, this will be the case. If so, make sure you present the information in that order. Secondly, if there is not an obviously logical order to the information, think about your material from the reader's point of view. What will it be most helpful for him to know about first? Is understanding one point dependent on knowing another? If so, make sure the information appears in that order. Finally, if you still cannot decide on the most appropriate order to present your information, try out several alternatives. Make two or three outlines each with the information in a different order. Does one of the outlines stand out as more effective than the others? Which of the outlines is most helpful to the reader?

In the case of a large report, you may want to divide up the evidence and findings into chapters or sections. This is especially helpful if the information falls naturally into several main sections. Dividing a large report into chapters helps both the writer and the reader. The chapters provide a logical framework for organizing the information and writing the report. They also provide the reader with some natural break points in his study of the report.

In any event, you should take care to present your information accurately and unambiguously. You should make sure that you explain the provenance of important pieces of information. For example, if you quote facts about the future growth rates in your industry, mention the source of the figures – perhaps a business school or industry association. By presenting the sources of your information in this kind of transparent way, you enhance the authority of your report.

Footnotes are a useful tool for referencing information. They enable you to provide detailed facts about the source of a piece of information without interrupting the flow of your argument. But use footnotes sparingly – not more than two or three to a page – or they become irritating to the reader.

- *Analysis.* When you have presented your evidence and findings, you move on to present an analysis of the information. Depending on the nature of the report, you may do this as you present the findings so that the evidence and the analysis are interwoven. Alternatively, you may prefer to present the evidence first and the analysis afterwards. It is often helpful to present the analysis separately when there is a large body of evidence. Another reason for presenting the analysis separately is when there is likely to be disagreement over the analysis – where the evidence can be interpreted in different ways. Keeping the analysis in one section (hopefully) confines the controversy to that section of the report.

  On the other hand, you may want to mix the analysis with the evidence if you want to guide your readers strongly to a particular point of view. If you take this route, you need to be certain it will be acceptable to your readers. It is certainly an effective approach when you are writing a report whose main purpose is to influence opinion or gain publicity, but may be less acceptable if the purpose of the report is to provide information or recommend a decision, where the readers may want the evidence and the analysis clearly separated.

- *Conclusions and recommendations.* Whereas analysis shows how you have interpreted the evidence, the conclusions show what you have decided or what you recommend on the basis of your analysis. The conclusions stand apart from the analysis so that your readers can see clearly what they are and decide whether to accept them. In most cases, you will present a single set of conclusions. In rarer cases, you may want to present alternative conclusions, especially if the subject matter of the report is controversial or if the evidence you have

53

assembled is inconclusive. In these cases, perhaps the buck does not stop on your desk, and the final decisions should be taken by more senior people.

Depending on size and subject matter, this section of your report may fall into two parts. In the first part you discuss your general conclusions. In the second part, you set out the recommendations. This is a workmanlike approach, because it avoids each recommendation becoming entangled in a large amount of justification. For example, do not write:

– In view of the over-crowding in the present office, and because of the need to expand the department, it is recommended that the accounts department moves to the new office building on 1 February 1995 and not 1 December 1994 as there is a possibility that the cabling for the new computers will not be completed.

Apart from the fact that the subordinate phrases obscure the recommendation, this approach also invites the reader to disagree with the central recommendation if he does not wholeheartedly agree with every supporting statement in the sentence. ('I think we will have the computer cabling completed by the first of December so let's move earlier.')

Ideally, each recommendation should be a single clear statement. For example, it is more effective to write:

– It is recommended that the accounts department moves to the new office building on 1 February 1995.

This presents the recommendation clearly, shorn of all its justification subtext. In any event, you have

argued the reasons for your recommendation else-
where in the report.

• *Appendices.* There is a huge range of appendices you
could include in a report, but the first point to consider is whether you should include any. Appendices can add substantially to the bulk of your report, but do they add much to the understanding of
the subject matter? In other words, are the appendices adding weight without insight? As a general
rule, only include an appendix if it adds useful extra
information that the reader needs in order to appreciate the conclusions and recommendations you
have reached.

Normally, an appendix will consist of a self-contained piece of information whose inclusion in the
main body of the report would have unnecessarily
diverted the reader at that point or held up the flow
of the narrative or argument. An example of information that could be included in an appendix is
an important piece of evidence which you considered in reaching your recommendations but
which you did not want to place in the main body of
the report. It could be a letter, a document or extract
from a document, a table of figures, the results of a
survey or many other things.

You should number every appendix and list each on
the contents page. You should also cross-reference
each from the main body of your text, when you
deal with an issue where it might be helpful for the
reader to glance at the relevant appendix.

• *Bibliography and sources of evidence.* You will not
normally include these in reports of modest size and
scope. However, in a large report, perhaps one
compiled by a working party, it might well be

relevant to include a list of people and organizations that gave evidence to the working party. You should divide the list into those who gave evidence in person and those who sent written evidence. If you have consulted a large number of books or other reports in compiling your report, it might be helpful to provide a bibliography for the reader. For each entry in the bibliography, you give the name of the book, the author(s), the publisher and the date of publication of the edition you consulted.

• *Index*. Again, the inclusion of an index is rare in a report, but it is something you might want to consider for a very large report – say one that runs to more than 100 pages. The index should refer not only to the people and organizations you mention in the report, but also the concepts you deal with. Study the indexes in quality non-fiction books in order to gain an idea of the different indexing styles available. Choose a style which indexes the report at the most appropriate level of detail.

REPORT WRITING STEP BY STEP

Drafting a report requires the same high level of writing skills needed for any important business document. For general advice about these skills, you should consult *Perfect Business Writing*, (Century Business) by the author of this book.

What about the specific skills of writing a report? How should you set about the task? You cannot begin to write your report until you clearly understand the conclusions and recommendations you wish to reach. Report writing is like setting off on a journey. You need to know where you are going before you depart. If you don't know where you are going, you will wander around and end up anywhere. Similarly, if you do not understand the conclusions and recommendations you want your report to reach, you will not be able to marshall the material you researched in order to support them. You will be writing without purpose or direction.

The golden rule of report writing, therefore, is: do not start writing until you know what your conclusions and recommendations will be and the reasons you have reached them. As we saw in chapter four, this means thoroughly thinking through your material either by yourself or discussing it with other members of your working party. When you have decided on your conclusions and recommendations you are in a position to start writing the report.

You should start writing the different sections of your report in this order:

- Introduction
- Findings and evidence
- Analysis
- Conclusions and recommendations

When you have written these sections, you should review them before you go on to write any more sections. Go back over your draft text and examine it with a critical eye. Ask yourself some hard questions. Does the introduction accurately describe what is to come – or does it make promises which are not fulfilled in the rest of the report? Have I included all the evidence that is relevant? Have I presented the evidence fairly? Have I given the correct weight to the most important evidence? Have I presented the evidence in the most effective order?

Next question your analysis. Is my analysis justified by the evidence? Have I gone farther than the evidence justifies? Have I overlooked important parts of the evidence? Do the different parts of my analysis hang coherently together or do I contradict myself?

Finally, study your conclusions and recommendations. Are my conclusions justified by my analysis? Is the link from evidence through analysis to conclusions clear in the case of every conclusion? Are my recommendations sensible and reasonable? Are any of the recommendations ambiguous? Have I expressed my recommendations clearly? Are these recommendations likely to be acceptable to the person or group which commissioned the report? If not, should I add extra evidence to support them and clearer analysis to punch home why I believe they are the correct recommendations?

When you have been through this exercise, you will probably want to redraft some of what you have written. You may even want to redraft all of it. Do this before writing any other parts of the report. When you have a second draft of the introduction, evidence, analysis, conclusions and recommendations, subject it again to the critical questioning described above. If you believe it passes, then it is time to draft the other parts of the report:

- Title
- Contents
- Summary

You should also add appendices, the source of evidence and bibliography (if applicable) and the index (if applicable). When you have done that, you need to look at the whole report again for a final check. Does the whole report serve the purpose for which it is intended? You should certainly trust your own judgement to answer this question, but it is also valuable to seek the opinions of trusted colleagues. Ask people whose judgement you respect and who will look at the report in the light of its purpose. Seek the views of people who are able to take the broader view rather than those whose only contribution will be to point out an errant comma on page 73.

Other people's views will certainly be valuable in helping you to make a judgement about the shape and wording of your final report. Indeed, you may want to make further changes based on their suggestions. But be in no doubt: if it is your report it must, ultimately, be your judgement which decides how the report is presented. So do not be talked into making changes you do not believe in. If challenged, you will find it hard to justify them at a later date.

Writing as a team

What happens if you are producing your report as the head of a working party? Does the whole team write the report? Definitely not. You should avoid the situation in which people sit round trying to draft the report sentence by sentence. The working party should appoint a rapporteur whose task will be to produce the different drafts of the report under the direction of the working party.

The working party should discuss each section of the report in sufficient detail for the rapporteur to have a clear idea of the consensus of the team. When the rapporteur has produced the first draft, the working party should discuss it in fairly general terms (no nit-picking detail at this stage) with a view to producing a second draft which more closely meets the working party's aims.

It is at second draft stage that the working party should go through the report paragraph by paragraph, making any fine adjustments that are needed. Then the rapporteur produces a third draft. At this stage, the report should be close to the finished version. It needs to be critically examined (perhaps by the working party chairman and the rapporteur) against the points mentioned above. As a result, the rapporteur may make some final changes. When the fourth and final draft of the report comes back to the working party, it should be in a form which the members can approve without further detailed discussion.

To summarize:

- Understand the different sections that could appear in a report and choose those most appropriate.
- Approach the drafting of a report in a logical way.
- Evaluate the first draft with a critical eye and redraft where necessary.
- Appoint a rapporteur to draft a report for a working party.

6

DESIGN, LAYOUT AND PRODUCTION

WORDS ON A PAGE

When all is said and done, your report ends up as words on a page. (True, there may be a few charts and diagrams, and we will come to those in a moment.) No matter how well researched the evidence, how wise the analysis and how compelling the conclusions, you will undermine it all if you do not present the information accessibly. This means the report must be easy to handle and straightforward to read. In other words, it must be fit for the purpose.

You need to think about this even before you start to write the text because some of the issues will affect how you approach the writing. It is possible that your organization has a house style for reports which deals with such issues as page layout, paragraph numbering and so on. If so, you need to obtain a copy of this house style and study it before you start writing. If not, you need to decide how to lay out the report before you start writing in order to ensure consistency of approach throughout the document.

One of the issues you need to consider is whether or not you will number the paragraphs and, if so, which numbering convention you will adopt. The point of paragraph numbering is to make it easier to refer to parts of the report during discussions. In a report of two or three pages, you might choose to dispense with paragraph numbering. In a longer report, it is essential to number paragraphs. There are three main numbering conventions to choose from:

- *Sequential numbering.* With this approach, you number the first paragraph 1, the second 2 and so on through the report. It has the advantage of being simple and straightforward. But it has some drawbacks. For example, it is not possible to show how a number of paragraphs are logically grouped together. Nor is it useful if you want to include sub-paragraphs within paragraphs.

- *Mixed numbers and letters.* With this approach, you number main paragraphs with arabic numerals and sub-paragraphs with lower case letters. You use roman numerals to pick out further divisions with sub-paragraphs. So numbering would proceed like this: 1 a i, 1 a ii, 1 b i, 2 a i, 2 b i, 2 b ii, etc. The advantage of this system is that it helps you to group information logically together and to make the different points stand out. In addition, by making a small indent for the lettered sub-paragraphs and a larger indent for roman numeral sub-paragraphs, you guide the eye down the page and provide visual variety, breaking up large slabs of text. However, this approach is not always suitable for a long report and it can become cumbersome if there is a large number of sub-paragraphs within paragraphs.

- *Decimal numbering.* With this approach, main paragraphs receive a number, first-level paragraphs a number after a first decimal point, and second-level paragraphs a number after a second decimal point. So numbering proceeds like this: 1.1.1, 1.1.2, 1.2.1, 1.3.1, 2.1.1, 2.1.2, etc. As with the mixed numbering and lettering approach, the same points about indenting apply. The advantage of this approach is that it is severely logical. But again, it is not necessarily suitable for really long reports for the same reasons as the mixed numbers and letters approach. In addition, it can prove confusing to implement in practice – should that paragraph be 12.2.3 or 12.3.2?

Charts, diagrams and pictures

Many reports could be greatly improved with the intelligent use of charts, diagrams and pictures. Yet too often writers overlook this potentially important ingredient of a report. Pictorial devices are most effective when they work with the text in order to help make a point more powerfully. They are least effective when the writer includes them for no other reason than that he thinks it makes the report look 'nicer'.

There are two kinds of charts that are especially useful in reports – those that illustrate relationships and those that illustrate ratios. Charts that illustrate relationships include:

- *Organization chart.* This is a chart that shows the relationship of one part of the organization to another. It generally consists of boxes linked by lines often (but not always) arranged in a nested hierarchy. The organization chart is effectively a high-level map of an organization.

- *Block diagram.* This is a generally simple chart which is often used to show the order in which activities must be carried out to complete a process. It consists of a start block, and number of blocks each of which represents a self-contained activity, and a stop block. The block diagram is an effective way of illustrating the workings of a process.

- *Flow chart.* There are several different types of flow chart. They are drawn using a library of standard shapes, where each shape represents a different type of activity – for example a decision or an action. A standard flowchart is used to show the relationship between the different activities in a business process. A functional flowchart also pictures the activities in a process but, in addition, shows how those activities move between different work units. A geographical flow chart shows how activities move between different geographical locations. All of these are valuable visual aids to help describe the workings of complex business processes.

Figure 1 An Organization Chart

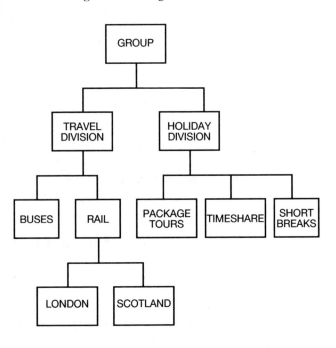

Charts that illustrate ratios are normally used to display numerical results and are common to reports. The main types are:

● *Graph.* Figures plotted against two axes – a horizontal time axis and vertical value axis. Straight lines link the intersection points. More than one line can be placed on the same graph. Different coloured

Figure 2 A Block Diagram

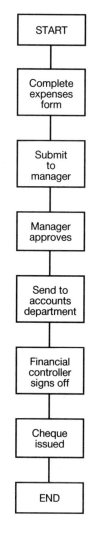

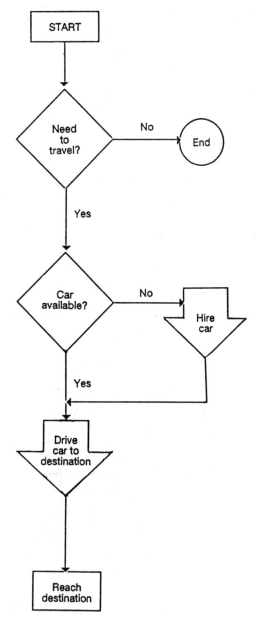

Figure 3 A simple process flowchart

lines can be used to show the relationships between different sets of figures – for example, this year's sales compared with last year's.

- *Histogram.* Otherwise known as a bar chart. The horizontal axis is used to plot the information type – for example, sales regions such as south, north, east and west. The vertical axis plots the amount. Bars of appropriate height are used to display the measure. Again, bars can be grouped together – for example in threes, to show last year's, budget and actual for each region. Different colours or shading helps to make the histogram easier to follow.

- *Pie chart.* This is used to show the proportions of a whole taken by each part. A circle is divided into slices, each slice in its correct ratio to the whole. A pie chart is often used in an annual report to show the proportion of turnover or profit earned by each division or subsidiary of the company.

- *Pictogram.* This displays numerical information with appropriate pictures which are used in proportion to the size of the numbers they represent. The pictures are usually displayed along a horizontal scale. For example, a pictogram showing the value of agricultural production in the UK might use pictures of pigs, cows, sheep, and so on to represent the different kinds of livestock. The number of pictures of each would be in proportion to the value of production.

Beyond these two categories of charts, there is a wide range of diagrams and other pictorial matter that might form part of your report. These could include maps, plans, drawings of equipment or apparatus, photographs, and so on. In deciding what pictorial matter to include be guided by three principles. First, does it advance the purpose of the report? Secondly, does it add value to the text? Thirdly, does it enhance the appearance of the report?

GETTING INTO PRINT

Finally, you must consider how the report is to be produced in multiple copies. You will need to give some preliminary thought to this at the outset because it could influence the way you produce the text. At the simplest level, you will produce just two copies of your report – one for yourself and one for the person who requested it. At higher levels, the report's circulation could run into hundreds, even thousands of copies.

Whether you choose to write the text in longhand and then have it keyboarded, or whether you keyboard it yourself, we start from the assumption that the text of your report exists on a word processor. (If the text doesn't exist on a word processor, you should certainly arrange to install one. Producing a report without a word processor is now rather like tilling a field with a horse-drawn plough.)

In many cases, you will be able to run off the text of the report direct from the word processor. In other cases, you may feel it needs to be presented in a more sophisticated format than pages of straight text. In which case, you should turn to desktop publishing. There are now a number of desktop publishing (DTP) computer programs available that allow you to produce pages of text to book publishing standards. Their drawback is that using the DTP programs skilfully is not quite as easy as the software companies would like you to believe. Unless you have already learned to use a DTP program, you probably need a specialist to handle the DTP element for you. Either you have somebody in house or you can use one of the DTP bureaux that have sprung up in most average-sized towns.

If having your report DTPed, don't just leave it to the bureau. You need to make it clear what you want the report to look like and you should be prepared to spend time with the DTP operator to work out trial page layouts and choose typefaces. The DTP operator will have a book of typefaces to choose from and will recommend faces that read well in blocks of text. Experiment with type sizes and line length until you achieve a combination that looks right on the page and reads easily.

Next, you need to decide the most effective way of producing the required number of copies of your report. There are three issues that will bear on your decision – the size of the report, the number of copies you plan to produce (the 'print run'), and whether the report contains any pictorial matter. There are three main options for producing your report:

- *Running the copies directly off your word processor's printer*. This is the best approach when you have a smallish report and require only a handful of copies. However, once you get above a total of, say, about 100 pages to print this approach becomes rather cumbersome.

- *Running a master copy off the word processor or DTP system and then photocopying (including specialist high-speed photocopying)*. This is an option for large reports of up to quite large runs, especially if high-speed copying services are used. For example, several hundred copies of a report of up to 200 or 300 pages could realistically be produced by a high-speed copying service at prices which are competitive with printing. There are now services which can take the text straight from a computer floppy disk and produce the finished reports. However, the main drawback of high-speed copying is that it does not give as high a quality as printing. This is especially true if the report contains complex diagrams or charts with large solid blocks.

- *Running a master copy off the DTP system and printing.* This is the option to choose when the report has to be produced to a high print quality (including possible photographs and diagrams) in large numbers. For smallish print runs, it is often the most expensive option but it produces the best results. However, for large print runs of any-sized report, printing is often the most economic option. If the standard of presentation is important – for example, in a report prepared to influence opinion – then printing is the choice to make.

Along with the method of printing, you also need to make a decision about the binding of the report. Again, your decision will be determined by the nature of the report. The options are:

- *Stapling.* The simplest approach for small reports with small circulations. A cheap and cheerful approach – and looks it – but perfectly acceptable for a wide range of internal reports. Becomes ineffective when reports get large and the staples don't go through all the sheets. Then consider:

- *Treasury tags.* Can hold together up to about 200 pages, depending on the length of the tag. But reports bound this way are not always easy to handle, especially if they are large – the pages slip about and tear loose from the tag.

- *Ready-made folders.* These come in a variety of formats available from your friendly neighbourhood stationer. They are often comparatively pricey – typically £1 or more a time – and sometimes not all that effective (especially the ones where you slide the pages of your report between a groove-shaped piece of plastic. Open the pages too wide and the whole thing falls apart.) However, if you have a small report and small print run, a ready made folder could provide the answer.

- *Comb-binding.* The left hand margin of each page is punched with a line of rectangular holes. Then a circular comb is inserted through them to hold the lot together – often with cardboard or acetate covers. You can buy machines to do this starting at about £300-£400. Alternatively, you can get your reports bound at any instant print shop which provides the service and most do. Comb binding is an excellent option for any report of about 30–300 pages as it makes the report comparatively easy to handle and is durable.

- *Binding.* This is the option to choose if your report has been printed. The report can be saddle-stitched – stapled or sewn down the central gutter between the centre left and right hand pages. Saddle stitching is suitable for reports of up to about 80 pages. Alternatively, you can choose perfect binding – where the pages are glued or stitched in groups at the spine so that the bound report assumes a block shape, like this book. Perfect binding is more expensive than saddle stitching but provides a higher quality result. However, perfect binding is generally impractical below about 32 pages.

To summarize:

- Consider the best way to lay out your text on the page for easy reading.
- Use diagrams and charts when they add value to the text.
- Select the most appropriate printing and binding methods for each report.

ANY OTHER BUSINESS

POST-REPORT MOVES

So you have completed and delivered your report. Is that it? Not entirely. Your report could be the ingredient needed to set off many different kinds of reactions. You need to be prepared. For this reason you should not sweep all your source material into the wastepaper basket the day after you deliver the report. You might need it again.

What could happen? You might be asked to provide further information on the report in general or a specific section of it. Alternatively, you might be asked to provide a follow-up report. You could be challenged to justify some of the conclusions or recommendations you have made in the report. You may even be asked to present the report's main findings to a meeting. These and other possibilities mean that you should continue to regard the report as a live project in your work schedule for a reasonable period after you have delivered it.

However, perhaps none of these things happen. Perhaps you hear nothing. Does that mean you can quietly forget the project? Preferably not. You should seek some feedback on the report from those who received it. Did it deal with the issues they wanted addressed? Did the report meet their expectations? Were there any issues not dealt with which they would have liked to be covered? Have they taken any decisions based on the report?

Information to questions such as these is important because it helps you to evaluate how successfully you completed the report project. No matter how many reports you write, there are always new lessons to learn.

You can learn from failures as well as successes. Why did they not act on the report? Did I present enough evidence? Was the argument logical and convincing? Were my recommendations realistic? Did they have a 'hidden agenda' which I failed to appreciate and account for in the report? Did the report fall victim to internal politics which I failed to appreciate and allow for? Was the report simply not as readable as it should have been? The report writer who continually improves asks questions such as these about any major report project.

It is easy to understand why a business manager regards the call for a report as just another chore. In fact, if you regard report writing as an unwelcome chore, you will probably not be very good at it. Your boredom and sense of tedium will tend to show through in the report. But the manager who gains a reputation for producing effective reports will help himself as well as his organization. Most managers, if pushed, can produce some sort of report, which perhaps just about fits the bill. But the manager that produces a report which stands out as well above average, stands out as above average himself. He marks himself in the eyes of his bosses as someone with a valuable and useful skill. The quality of his thinking also shows through in the report – and that can commend itself to his bosses as well. In short, the writer of quality reports is doing no harm to his career prospects.

Six steps to success

What benchmarks can you use against which to judge the success of a report? If your report can measure up to the following six qualities, it should be as close to perfect as you can make it.

- *Actionable*. There are many purposes for a report but, in most cases, the recipient of the report will want to take some kind of action based on its contents. So the successful report presents information in a way that guides the reader to action. There are several ways it can do this – for example, by providing clear and sensible recommendations. In an actionable report, the information is organized so that the reader can immediately see those issues that require action and those which provide background. The tone and style of an actionable report is upbeat. It reinforces the reader's confidence to take the decisions that are needed.

- *Tailored.* A report can, conceivably, have a readership of one or one million. Whichever the number, in the tailored report information is organized to make it accessible and relevant to the readership. This involves the writer tailoring both the information and the style in which it is written to the readers. In the case of some reports – for example, regular reports containing performance information – it may involve tailoring the report to an exact specification laid down by the reader. In all cases, a well tailored report will make the reader say: 'This is just what I need.'

- *Focus.* The focus comes from a clear understanding of the purpose of the report. Focus means addressing that purpose in every page and every paragraph. In a well focused report, all the information is assembled to support the main purpose of the report. The narrative or argument of the report drives forward steadily from page to page. There are no time-wasting digressions. Background information is kept to the minimum needed to provide the reader with enough understanding of the subject. The purpose of the report shines through from the first sentence to the last.

- *Timely.* A successful report is delivered on time. This may seem obvious, but plenty of reports arrive on the reader's desk too late to be useful. If the report is to be used as the basis of a decision, the reader needs a reasonable time to study it before he takes the decision. How long depends both on the length of the report and the complexity and importance of the decisions. Many people may have to discuss the report before they take the decision. That is a potentially lengthy process. It is the job of the report writer to present the report in plenty of time so that the decision-making process is not rushed.

- *Organized.* In a successful report the contents are carefully and helpfully organized. The information is divided into logical sections, an appropriate paragraph numbering system helps the reader to reference the information, illuminating charts and diagrams are provided wherever they add value to the text. Often, an organized report is the output of an organized report project. If the writer approaches his task logically, conducts his research systematically and thoroughly, writes his report carefully, the sense of organization will show through in the finished report. Muddle begets muddle – and it shows.

- *Reliable.* Finally, a successful report inspires confidence. It possesses the five qualities mentioned above. The reader can sense the authority of the report radiating off its pages. It gives him confidence to take decisions – perhaps important decisions – based on its contents.

Reports in the computer age
So far in this book, we have discussed reports as paper documents. Increasingly, they will be electronic 'documents' in a computer. As we have already mentioned, most reports are now written on word processors. If a report is written on a computer, it is only a short step to

reading it on a computer. Admittedly, it will be a long time before managers want to read a long document on a workstation because that can prove rather tiring to the eyes. And a paper document is more portable – it can be read on the plane or train – although the growing acceptance of 'laptop' computers is even undermining that argument.

However, the computer presents all kinds of report producing possibilities that paper never had. For example, reports can be assembled more quickly from information already held in databases. Using report generation software, it is possible to pull different kinds of information out of different databases and then combine it in a new format in a single report. Computer graphics help the report writer to produce full colour graphics more cheaply and more easily than was ever the case before.

Not far away is the prospect of the computer-based 'multimedia' report. This will use special software to allow the report compiler to include text, graphics, photographs, motion video and voice in a report which the viewer can access from his own workstation. For the manager clever enough to spot the opportunity and master the technology, multimedia offers the prospect of producing exciting new types of reports which can present information in a far more compelling way than ever before.

Like most other aspects of the business world, the report, too, will undergo dramatic transformation. But despite changes in technology, most of the principles of report production remain the same. Even a report produced with the latest glitzy technology and the most exciting visual effects will fail if it does not serve the purpose for which it is intended.

In the end, it is human judgement which will be the

most important ingredient in reports. And that will be as precious a commodity as ever.

To summarize:

- Keep your background information for a reasonable period after delivering a report.
- Understand the six factors that make a successful report.
- Investigate the potential of computers to deliver new kinds of reports.

PERFECT BUSINESS WRITING

Peter Bartram

In every job, writing plays a part – and the ability to write well helps you to perform your job better. Good writing is important both for you and for your organization. It enables you to communicate effectively with your colleagues. It advances your career prospects. It contributes to the success of your company by improving communication with customers and suppliers – and it enhances the corporate image.

If you, like so many people, lack confidence in your writing ability, this book is the perfect answer.

£5.99 Net in the UK only.

ISBN 0-7126-5534-4

PERFECT TIME MANAGEMENT

Ted Johns

Managing your time effectively means adding value to
everything you do. This book will help you to master
the techniques and skills essential to grasping control of
your time and your life.

If you can cut down the time you spend meeting people,
talking on the 'phone, writing and reading business
papers and answering subordinates' questions, you can
use the time saved for creative work and the really important elements of your job. Learn how to deal with
interruptions, manage the boss and cut down on meetings time – above all, how to minimize paperwork.
You'll be amazed how following a few simple guide-
lines will improve the quality of both your working life
and your leisure time.

£5.99 Net in UK only.

ISBN 0-7126-5549-2

THE PERFECT BUSINESS PLAN

Ron Johnson

A really professional business plan is crucial to success. This book provides a planning framework and shows you how to complete it for your own business in 100 easy to follow stages.

Business planning will help you to make better decisions today, taking into account as many of the relevant factors as possible. A carefully prepared business plan is essential to the people who will put money into the business, to those who will lend it money, and above all to the people who carry out its day to day management.

£5.99 Net in UK only.

ISBN 0-7126-5524-7

THE PERFECT NEGOTIATION

Gavin Kennedy

The ability to negotiate effectively is a vital skill required in business and everyday situations.

Whether you are negotiating over a business deal, a pay rise, a difference of opinion between manager and staff, or the price of a new house or car, this invaluable book, written by one of Europe's leading experts in negotiation, will help you to get a better deal every time, and avoid costly mistakes.

£5.99 Net in UK only.

ISBN 0-7126-5465-8

THE PERFECT PRESENTATION

Andrew Leigh and Michael Maynard

When everything seems to go right, you perform at your absolute best, your audience reacts enthusiastically and comes away inspired, then you've given the perfect presentation!

But success is underpinned by hard work, and the authors of this book provide the necessary framework on which to base your presentations, under the headings of the 'Five Ps': Preparation, Purpose, Presence, Passion and Personality.

Many major organizations have used material from the courses on which this book is based. Now you can gain those benefits – at a fraction of the cost.

£5.99 Net in UK only.

ISBN 0-7126-5536-0

THE PERFECT APPRAISAL

Howard Hudson

Implementing the right appraisal scheme can significantly improve employee and company performance.

Most companies have some form of appraisal scheme in place, yet they get very little out of it. A properly conducted appraisal scheme can raise performance standards, cut costs and in some cases 'revolutionize' the business. This concise and invaluable handbook provides managers and organizations with a practical blueprint for appraisal, and shows how they can obtain maximum benefit from appraisal schemes.

£5.99 Net in UK only
ISBN 0-7126-5541-7

THE PERFECT DISMISSAL

John McManus

Dismissals are wretched occasions for everybody concerned; but unhappiness and unpleasantness can be kept to an absolute minimum by the use of this book.

It tells both employer and employee how to avoid legal pitfalls and their associated costs. Just as importantly, it emphasizes human considerations – common sense, fairness and the dignity of the individual.

The Perfect Dismissal provides a clear and well-balanced summary of a complex subject.

£5.99 Net in UK only.

ISBN 0-7126-5641-3